HOW TO MIX
100
Cocktails

by 'Bernard'

foulsham
LONDON NEW YORK TORONTO SYDNEY

foulsham

Bennetts Close, Cippenham, Berkshire SL1 5AP

ISBN 0-572-01775-8

Printed in Great Britain by
Cox & Wyman Ltd, Reading, Berkshire

CONTENTS

PREFACE

The writer of this book has, for many years, made a habit of jotting down the recipe of every cocktail that he has come across, which possessed special merit. The present compilation of well over a hundred recipes is the result of his notes.

As he has travelled in various parts of the world and has gathered the recipes from far and wide, the collection is more or less unique.

COCKTAILS

All of which are alcoholic

How the dictionaries define a cocktail, I do not know; but, were I asked, I should say that it was a delicate combination of ingredients, all of which contribute their share in building up a unique beverage, possessing an individualism of its own.

Whether the reader agrees with me or not hardly matters. What does matter is that he should appreciate that the ingredients of a cocktail have been thought out and selected by a master-mind who has blended them together to obtain a definite flavour. Thus, to alter them, in substance or quantity, will surely alter the resulting effect and, generally, an alteration means an inferior result.

Having stressed the need for keeping faithfully to the recipes, as printed, the next point to note is that it is advisable to put the ingredients together in the order that they appear in the recipes. Sometimes it is essential and, if the habit is formed, there will never be any mistakes.

For your cocktail bar, a certain number of implements are, more or less, necessary. They may be enumerated as follows:

•A SHAKER. This consists of two metal plated containers which fit one in the other. The contrivance is held in both hands and shaken up and down until the ingredients are thoroughly mixed.

Other types of shakers, for which it was claimed no ice was needed, have appeared on the market, but presumably were not successful, since they are no longer attainable.

•A STRAINER. This is composed of a metal ring, covered with gauze, and a handle attached. After the ingredients have been shaken or stirred, the mixture is poured through it to strain out the chips of ice, fruit pulp, etc.

•A MIXING GLASS. This is merely a large tumbler or bar glass, into which the ingredients are put when they are to be stirred. Note, here, that some liquids, such as champagne, must not be shaken or they will lose their natural effervescence. Such liquids are stirred in the mixing glass.

•A MIXING SPOON. This is a spoon holding about the same amount as a teaspoon, but with a very long handle. It makes stirring easy.

•A BUNDLE OF COCKTAIL STICKS to permit the simple manipulation of cherries, olives, etc., which are often served with cocktails.

•A SUPPLY OF DRINKING STRAWS

•A CORKSCREW AND BOTTLE OPENER

Though the above outfit is required for any cocktail bar, there are certain things needed far more, and they are the drinks themselves. A well-appointed bar should stock the following:

PERNOD	GIN
ANGOSTURA BITTERS	RED PORT
BRANDY	RUM
BROWN CURAÇAO	SCOTCH WHISKY
CALVADOS	SHERRY

CANADIAN CLUB WHISKY
CHAMPAGNE
DUBONNET
FRENCH VERMOUTH
GRENADINE SYRUP
ITALIAN VERMOUTH
MARASCHINO
ORANGE BITTERS
PLAIN SYRUP

With the above ingredients on hand, ninety per cent of the alcoholic recipes in this book can be compounded, if such oddments as sprigs of mint and cherries are not counted. Lots of recipes call for lemon or orange peel juice; just twist a strip of peel over the glass to add a dash of juice to the cocktail.

Now a word about the glasses in which the drinks should be served:

1. A COCKTAIL GLASS holds about 75ml (2 ½ fl oz) of liquid.
2. A SMALL WINE GLASS holds about 100ml (4 fl oz).
3. A LARGE WINE GLASS holds about 150ml (¼ pint).
4. A TUMBLER holds about 300ml (½ pint).
5. A SHERBET GLASS is like a small tumbler.
6. A LIQUEUR GLASS holds about 40ml (1¼ fl oz).
7. A SUNDAE GLASS is bowl-shaped and is useful when serving fruit cocktails.

Remember:
    1 part equals 25ml (5tsp) or ⅙ gill
    6 parts equals 150ml (¼ pint) or 1 gill

PERNOD

1 dash of ANGOSTURA BITTERS
1½ parts PERNOD
2 dashes of ANISETTE (or PLAIN
    SYRUP)
1 part WATER
1 dash of LEMON PEEL JUICE
1 CHERRY
¾ tumblerful of broken ICE

Three-quarters fill a tumbler with broken Ice and add the Angostura Bitters. Then put in the Pernod, Anisette and Water. Shake well and pass through a strainer into a cocktail glass. Serve with a dash of Lemon Peel Juice on top and with a Cherry.

    For anyone who knows little of cocktails, this is an excellent one to try at the outset.

ADAM'S APPLE

---

1 ½ parts CALVADOS
¾ part ITALIAN VERMOUTH
¾ part GIN
2 dashes of YELLOW CHARTREUSE
1 CHERRY
1 dash of LEMON PEEL JUICE
½ tumblerful of broken ICE

Half fill a tumbler with broken Ice. Then add the Calvados, Italian Vermouth, Gin and Yellow Chartreuse. Stir well and pass through a strainer into a cocktail glass. Serve with a Cherry and a dash of Lemon Peel Juice on top.

A fairly strong cocktail.

ALCAZAR

1 ½ parts CANADIAN CLUB WHISKY
1 part BENEDICTINE
1 CHERRY
1 or 2 dashes of ORANGE PEEL JUICE
½ tumblerful of broken ICE

Half fill a tumbler with broken Ice. Then add the Canadian Club Whisky and Benedictine. Stir well and pass through a strainer into a cocktail glass. Serve with a Cherry and a dash of Orange Peel Juice on top.

If desired, a small dash of Orange Bitters may be included in the above.

APPLEJACK

1 dash of ANGOSTURA BITTERS
2 parts CALVADOS
1 teaspoon BROWN CURACAO
1 CHERRY
1 dash of LEMON PEEL JUICE
½ tumblerful of broken ICE

Half fill a tumbler with broken Ice and add the Angostura Bitters. Then add the Calvados and Brown Curaçao. Stir up and pass through a strainer into a cocktail glass. Serve with a Cherry and a dash of Lemon Peel Juice on top.

Orange Bitters can be used instead of Angostura Bitters, if preferred.

Calvados is the continental name for Applejack Brandy.

BACARDI

1 ½ parts BACARDI
1 ½ parts LIME JUICE
2 dashes of GRENADINE SYRUP
1 CHERRY
½ tumblerful of broken ICE

Half fill a tumbler with broken Ice and add the Bacardi. Then add the Lime Juice and Grenadine Syrup. Stir well and pass through a strainer into a cocktail glass. Serve with a Cherry.

A very pleasant cocktail. This drink is very popular in America.

BAMBOO 1

½ teaspoon ORANGE BITTERS
1 ½ parts DRY SHERRY
1 ½ parts FRENCH VERMOUTH
1 dash of LEMON PEEL JUICE
½ tumblerful of broken ICE

Half fill a tumbler with broken Ice and add the Orange Bitters. Then add the Dry Sherry and French Vermouth. Stir well, strain and serve in a cocktail glass with a dash of Lemon Peel Juice on top.

BAMBOO 2

½ teaspoon ORANGE BITTERS
2 parts DRY SHERRY
1 part ITALIAN VERMOUTH
1 dash of LEMON PEEL JUICE
½ tumblerful of broken ICE

This cocktail is made up in exactly the same way as the previous one; but Italian Vermouth is used instead of French Vermouth. This makes the flavour much sweeter and, in our experience, it is preferred by women.

BENNETT

2 parts GIN
1 part LEMON or LIME JUICE
1 teaspoon ANGOSTURA BITTERS
½ shakerful of broken ICE

Half fill the shaker with broken Ice and add the Gin. Then add the Lemon and Lime Juice and the Angostura Bitters. Shake well and pass through a strainer into a cocktail glass.

This drink is very popular in South America.

BEVERLY HILLS

2 dashes of ANGOSTURA BITTERS
3 parts CALVADOS
1 CHERRY
1 dash of LEMON PEEL JUICE
½ tumblerful of broken ICE

The tumbler is half filled with broken Ice and the Angostura Bitters added. Then add the Calvados. Stir well and pass through a strainer into a cocktail glass. Serve with a Cherry and a dash of Lemon Peel Juice on top.

This cocktail is named after the famous town near Hollywood, California.

BIG BOY

1 teaspoon ANGOSTURA BITTERS
¾ part FRENCH VERMOUTH
¾ part ITALIAN VERMOUTH
1 ½ parts GIN
1 teaspoon ABSINTHE
1 CHERRY
1 dash of LEMON PEEL JUICE
½ tumblerful of broken ICE

Half fill a tumbler with broken Ice and add the Angostura Bitters. Then add the French Vermouth, Italian Vermouth, Gin and Absinthe. Stir up and pass through a strainer into a cocktail glass. Serve with a Cherry and a dash of Lemon Peel Juice on top.

A very pleasant cocktail which is also fairly strong.

BIJOU

¾ part DRY GIN
¾ part GREEN CHARTREUSE
¾ part ITALIAN VERMOUTH
½ teaspoon ORANGE BITTERS
1 dash of LEMON PEEL JUICE
1 CHERRY
½ tumblerful of broken ICE

Half fill a tumbler with broken Ice and add the Dry Gin. Then add the Green Chartreuse, Italian Vermouth and Orange Bitters. Stir well and pass through a strainer into a cocktail glass. Serve with a dash of Lemon Peel Juice on top and with a Cherry.

For those who enjoy something mild. Some people prefer to leave out the Orange Bitters.

BLACKTHORN 1

1 teaspoon PERNOD
½ teaspoon ANGOSTURA BITTERS
1 ½ parts FRENCH VERMOUTH
1 ½ parts SCOTCH WHISKY
1 dash of LEMON PEEL JUICE
½ tumblerful of broken ICE

Half fill a tumbler with broken Ice and add the Pernod. Then add the Angostura Bitters, French Vermouth and Scotch Whisky. Stir well and pass through a strainer into a wine glass. Serve with a dash of Lemon Peel Juice on top.

BLACKTHORN 2

½ teaspoon ORANGE BITTERS
1 dash of ANGOSTURA BITTERS
1 part SCOTCH WHISKY
1 part FRENCH VERMOUTH
1 part ITALIAN VERMOUTH
1 CHERRY
½ tumblerful of broken ICE

This cocktail is made up in the same way as the previous one except that Orange Bitters and Italian Vermouth are added and the Pernod is left out.

The flavour is not quite so subtle as the previous one.

BLACKTHORN 3

1 dash of ANGOSTURA BITTERS
1 dash of ORANGE BITTERS
1 part ITALIAN VERMOUTH
2 parts SLOE GIN
1 dash of LEMON PEEL JUICE
½ tumblerful of broken ICE

Make up as in the previous case. Sloe Gin is used in place of Scotch Whisky and the French Vermouth is left out. A more mellow flavour than the previous.

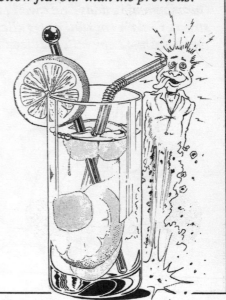

BRANDY 1

1 dash of PERNOD
10 drops of ANGOSTURA BITTERS
1 teaspoon BROWN CURACAO
2 parts BRANDY
1 CHERRY
1 dash of LEMON PEEL JUICE
½ tumblerful of broken ICE

Half fill a tumbler with Ice chips and add the dash of Pernod. Next add the Angostura Bitters, Brown Curaçao and Brandy. Stir well and pass through a strainer into a cocktail glass. Serve with a Cherry and a dash of Lemon Peel Juice on top.

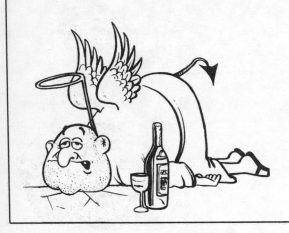

BRANDY 2

1 ½ parts BRANDY
1 ½ parts FRENCH VERMOUTH
1 dash of LEMON PEEL JUICE
1 CHERRY
½ tumblerful of broken ICE

This cocktail is made up in exactly the same way as the previous one. Use French Vermouth instead of the Pernod, the Angostura Bitters and the Curaçao. This makes a delightful variation.

A simpler cocktail to make than the previous one.

BRAZIL

1 dash of ORANGE BITTERS
1 ½ parts DRY SHERRY
1 ½ parts FRENCH VERMOUTH
1 dash of PLAIN SYRUP
2 dashes of PERNOD
1 dash of LEMON PEEL JUICE
½ tumblerful of broken ICE

The tumbler is half filled with broken Ice and the Orange Bitters added. Then add the Dry Sherry, French Vermouth, Plain Syrup and Pernod. Stir well, strain and serve in a cocktail or small wine glass with a dash of Lemon Peel Juice on top.

This is a very pleasant cocktail of medium strength.

BROADWAY

Few drops of ORANGE BITTERS
1 ½ parts ITALIAN VERMOUTH
3 parts DRY GIN
1 dash of ORANGE PEEL JUICE
½ shakerful of broken ICE

Half fill the shaker with broken Ice and add the Orange Bitters. Then put in the Italian Vermouth and Dry Gin. Shake well and pass through a strainer into a small wine glass. Serve with a dash of Orange Peel Juice on top.

This cocktail is very popular in New York.

BRONX

1 part DRY GIN
½ part ITALIAN VERMOUTH
½ part FRENCH VERMOUTH
1 tablespoon ORANGE JUICE
1 dash of ORANGE BITTERS
½ shakerful of broken ICE

Half fill the shaker with broken Ice and then, in the following order, put in the Dry Gin, Italian Vermouth, French Vermouth, Orange Juice and Orange Bitters. Shake well and pass through a strainer into a cocktail glass.

Some connoisseurs prefer the above without the Orange Bitters They say that it gives a smoother flavour.

BUZZER

2 dashes of ANGOSTURA BITTERS
1 ½ parts DRY GIN
1 ½ parts ITALIAN VERMOUTH
1 teaspoon CREME DE MENTHE
1 CHERRY
½ shakerful of broken ICE

The shaker is half filled with broken Ice and the Angostura Bitters added. Then add the Dry Gin, Italian Vermouth and Crème de Menthe. Shake well and pass through a strainer into a cocktail glass. Serve with a Cherry.

A pleasant and fairly strong cocktail.

CHAMPAGNE 1

6 parts CHAMPAGNE
Few drops of BROWN CURACAO
Few drops of OLD BRANDY
Few drops of PLAIN SYRUP
½ tumblerful of broken ICE

When making this or any other Champagne Cocktail, be careful to have a bottle of Champagne on ice, and to keep it well corked. About 6 to 8 cocktails can be made with a bottle of Champagne.

An ordinary wine glass is best for measuring the drink. It is prepared in a tumbler half filled with broken Ice. Add the Brown Curaçao, Old Brandy, Plain Syrup and the Champagne in the above order. Stir well and serve in a large wine glass.

CHAMPAGNE 2

1 small lump of SUGAR
3 or 4 dashes of ANGOSTURA BITTERS
The juice of ¼ LEMON
4 ½ parts CHAMPAGNE
1 slice of LEMON
1 small piece of ICE

Soak the lump of Sugar in the Angostura Bitters. Squeeze the juice of ¼ Lemon into a wine glass and add the saturated Sugar. Then add the piece of Ice and fill up with the Champagne. Serve with a slice of Lemon. This is an admirable pick-me-up.

CHEERIO

1 dash of ORANGE BITTERS
1 tablespoon ORANGE JUICE
½ part ITALIAN VERMOUTH
½ part FRENCH VERMOUTH
1 part DRY GIN
2 dashes of PERNOD
½ shakerful of broken ICE

Half fill the shaker with broken Ice and add the Orange Bitters. Then add the Orange Juice, Italian Vermouth, French Vermouth, Dry Gin and Pernod. Shake well and pass through a strainer into a cocktail glass.

Many people prefer to add the Pernod afterwards and not to put it in the shaker.

Tangerine juice can be used instead of Orange juice. This makes a pleasant variation.

CHERRY

½ teaspoon ANGOSTURA BITTERS
1 teaspoon GRENADINE SYRUP
3 parts SCOTCH WHISKY
1 CHERRY
1 dash of LEMON PEEL JUICE
½ tumblerful of broken ICE

The tumbler is half filled with broken Ice and the Angostura Bitters is added. Then add the Grenadine Syrup and Whisky. Stir well and pass through a strainer into a wine glass. Serve with a Cherry and a dash of Lemon Peel Juice on top.

CHICAGO

Few drops of ANGOSTURA BITTERS
1 or 2 dashes of BROWN CURACAO
1 ½ parts BRANDY
1 ½ parts CHAMPAGNE
1 dash of LEMON JUICE
1 teaspoon powdered SUGAR
1 piece of LEMON PEEL
½ tumblerful of broken ICE

Half fill a tumbler with broken Ice and add the Angostura Bitters. Next add the Brown Curaçao, Brandy and Champagne. Stir well. Before serving, moisten the inside of a cocktail glass with the Lemon Juice and sprinkle with Sugar. Then strain the mixture into the cocktail glass and serve with a small piece of Lemon Peel on top.

CHOCOLATE

The yolk of a fresh EGG
1 ½ parts RED PORT
1 teaspoon CHOCOLATE POWDER
½ tumblerful of broken ICE

Half fill a tumbler with broken ICE and add the yolk of an Egg. Then add the Red Port and Chocolate Powder. Stir well and pass through a strainer into a wine glass.

Some people like to add 1 or 2 dashes of Yellow Chartreuse as well; but this is entirely optional.

CLOVER CLUB 1

The white of an EGG
The juice of a LEMON
1 teaspoon GRENADINE SYRUP
3 parts DRY GIN
1 dash of grated NUTMEG
½ shakerful of broken ICE

Half fill the shaker with broken Ice and add the white of an Egg. Then add the Lemon Juice, Grenadine Syrup and Dry Gin. Shake well and pass through a strainer into a cocktail glass containing a dash of Nutmeg.

Raspberry Syrup can be used instead of Grenadine Syrup, if desired. Be careful not to over-do the Nutmeg.

CLOVER CLUB 2

1 ½ parts DRY GIN
¾ part FRENCH VERMOUTH
1 teaspoon GRENADINE SYRUP
The juice of a LEMON
The white of an EGG
½ shakerful of broken ICE

This cocktail is made in exactly the same way as the previous one but with the addition of French Vermouth. This makes the cocktail much drier. See also Royal Clover Cocktail on page 97.

CLOVER LEAF

3 parts DRY GIN
1 teaspoon GRENADINE SYRUP
The juice of a LEMON
The white of an EGG
2 sprigs of MINT
½ shakerful of broken ICE

This is much the same as the Clover Club Cocktails, but the sprigs of Mint make a subtle difference to the flavour.

CLUB

12 drops of ANGOSTURA BITTERS
1 dash of GRENADINE
2 parts CANADIAN CLUB WHISKY
1 CHERRY
1 dash of LEMON PEEL JUICE
½ tumblerful of broken ICE

A tumbler is half filled with broken Ice and the Angostura Bitters is added. Then add the Grenadine and Canadian Club Whisky. Stir well and pass through a strainer into a cocktail glass. Serve with a Cherry and a dash of Lemon Peel Juice.

This cocktail is very popular and is of medium strength.

COFFEE

The yolk of an EGG
½ teaspoon SUGAR
1 ½ parts PORT
¾ part BRANDY
½ shakerful of ICE

Half fill the shaker with Ice chips and add the yolk of an Egg. Then add the Sugar, Port and Brandy. Shake until cold and pass through a strainer into a wine glass.

This cocktail is quite mild in flavour. It is a favourite with the ladies.

COOPERSTOWN 1

2 parts DRY GIN
1 part ITALIAN VERMOUTH
½ teaspoon ORANGE BITTERS
2 or 3 sprigs of MINT
1 or 2 dashes of LEMON PEEL JUICE
½ tumblerful of broken ICE

Half fill a tumbler with Ice chips and add the Dry Gin. Then add the Italian Vermouth, Orange Bitters and sprigs of Mint. Stir well and pass through a strainer into a cocktail glass. Serve with 1 or 2 dashes of Lemon Peel Juice on top.

COOPERSTOWN 2

¾ part FRENCH VERMOUTH
¾ part ITALIAN VERMOUTH
1 ½ parts DRY GIN
2 or 3 sprigs of MINT
1 or 2 dashes of LEMON PEEL JUICE
½ tumblerful of broken ICE

This cocktail is much the same as the previous recipe, but French Vermouth is used to obtain a drier flavour. The Orange Bitters is omitted.

CORONATION 1

1 teaspoon PEPPERMINT
1 teaspoon PEACH BITTERS
2 teaspoons RED CURACAO
2 parts OLD BRANDY
1 slice of LEMON
½ tumblerful of broken ICE

Half fill a tumbler with broken Ice. Put in the following order the Peppermint, Peach Bitters, Red Curaçao and Old Brandy. Stir well and pass through a strainer into a cocktail glass. Serve with a slice of Lemon on top.

Reduce the quantity of Curaçao, if a cocktail of medium strength is preferred.

CORONATION 2

1 ½ parts **FRENCH VERMOUTH**
1 ½ parts **SHERRY**
1 teaspoon **MARASCHINO**
1 teaspoon **ANGOSTURA BITTERS**
½ shakerful of broken **ICE**

Half fill the shaker with broken Ice and add the French Vermouth. Then add the Sherry, Maraschino and Angostura Bitters. Shake well and strain into a cocktail glass.

Some experts add Dubonnet instead of the Angostura Bitters and Maraschino. It provides a good variation and also makes an excellent aperitif.

40

DAIQUIRI

---

2 parts LIME JUICE
1 part RUM
1 or 2 dashes of GRENADINE
½ shakerful of broken ICE

Half fill the shaker with broken Ice and add the Lime Juice. Then add the Rum and Grenadine. Shake well and pass through a strainer into a cocktail glass.

This is quite a mild cocktail.

DAYDREAM

---

1 teaspoon BROWN CURACAO
1 teaspoon ANGOSTURA BITTERS
2 parts BRANDY
1 teaspoon MARASCHINO
1 dash of CHAMPAGNE
1 dash of LEMON PEEL JUICE
1 CHERRY
½ tumblerful of broken ICE

Half fill a tumbler with broken Ice and add the Brown Curaçao. Then put in the Angostura Bitters, Brandy and Maraschino. Stir well and pass through a strainer into a cocktail glass. Serve with a dash of Champagne, a dash of Lemon Peel Juice and a Cherry.

Pineapple Syrup can be used instead of Maraschino, if desired.

DEAUVILLE

3 parts DRY GIN
2 dashes of LIME JUICE
2 dashes of PLAIN SYRUP
1 dash of LEMON PEEL JUICE
½ shakerful of broken ICE

Half fill the shaker with broken Ice and add the Dry Gin. Then add the Lime Juice and Plain Syrup. Shake well and pass through a strainer into a cocktail glass. Serve with a dash of Lemon Peel Juice on top.

This cocktail is very popular with the ladies.

DEEP SEA

1 ½ parts DRY GIN
1 ½ parts FRENCH VERMOUTH
½ teaspoon PERNOD
½ teaspoon ORANGE BITTERS
1 OLIVE
1 dash of LEMON PEEL JUICE
½ shakerful of ICE chips

The shaker is half filled with Ice chips and the Dry Gin added. Then add the French Vermouth, Pernod and Orange Bitters. Shake well and pass through a strainer into a small wine glass. Serve with an Olive and a dash of Lemon Peel Juice on top.

This cocktail is of medium strength.

DEMPSEY

½ teaspoon PERNOD
1 dash of GRENADINE
2 parts BRANDY
1 part DRY GIN
½ shakerful of broken ICE

Half fill the shaker with broken Ice and add the Pernod. Then put in the Grenadine, Brandy and Dry Gin. Shake up and pass through a strainer into a cocktail glass.

A cocktail with plenty of 'kick' in it.

DEVIL'S

---

1 part PEPPERMINT
2 parts OLD BRANDY
½ shakerful of broken ICE

Half fill the shaker with broken Ice and add the Peppermint. Then add the Old Brandy. Shake up and pass through a strainer into a cocktail glass.

This cocktail is quite strong. Not for beginners.

DIABOLO

¾ part BROWN CURACAO
¾ part FRENCH VERMOUTH
1 ½ parts BRANDY
½ teaspoon ANGOSTURA BITTERS
1 CHERRY
1 dash of LEMON PEEL JUICE
½ tumblerful of broken ICE

Half fill a tumbler with the broken Ice and add the Brown Curaçao. Then add the French Vermouth, Brandy and Angostura Bitters. Shake well and pass through a strainer into a cocktail glass. Serve with a Cherry and a dash of Lemon Peel Juice.
This cocktail has plenty of 'kick' in it.

DIAMOND

1 part RUM
1 part GIN
1 part BROWN CURACAO
1 dash of LEMON PEEL JUICE
½ tumblerful of broken ICE

The tumbler should be half filled with broken Ice and the Rum added. Then add the Gin and Brown Curaçao. Shake well and strain into a cocktail glass. Serve with a dash of Lemon Peel Juice.

A fairly strong cocktail. It is not everybody's choice.

DIPLOMAT

1 ½ parts FRENCH VERMOUTH
¾ part ITALIAN VERMOUTH
¾ part PINEAPPLE SYRUP
1 dash of LEMON PEEL JUICE
1 CHERRY
½ tumblerful of broken ICE

Half fill a tumbler with broken Ice and add the French Vermouth. Then add the Italian Vermouth and Pineapple Syrup. Stir up and pass through a strainer into a cocktail glass. Serve with a dash of Lemon Peel Juice and a Cherry. A fairly mild cocktail.

DUBONNET

1 part DRY GIN
2 parts DUBONNET
½ teaspoon ORANGE BITTERS
½ shakerful of broken ICE

The shaker is half filled with broken Ice and the Dry Gin is added. Next add the Dubonnet and Orange Bitters. Shake up and pass through a strainer into a cocktail glass. This is a very good aperitif.

FIOUPE

1 part BRANDY
1 part ITALIAN VERMOUTH
2 or 3 dashes of BENEDICTINE
1 CHERRY
1 or 2 dashes of LEMON PEEL JUICE
½ tumblerful of broken ICE

Half fill a tumbler with broken Ice and add the Brandy. Next add the Italian Vermouth and Bénédictine. Stir up and pass through a strainer into a cocktail glass. Serve with a Cherry and 1 or 2 dashes of Lemon Peel Juice on top.

This cocktail has plenty of 'kick' in it.

FIRE DEVIL

2 dashes of ANGOSTURA BITTERS
1 ½ parts SLOE GIN
¾ part FRENCH VERMOUTH
¾ part ITALIAN VERMOUTH
1 dash of LEMON PEEL JUICE
½ tumblerful of broken ICE

The tumbler is half filled with broken Ice and the Angostura Bitters added. Now put in the Sloe Gin, French Vermouth and Italian Vermouth. Stir up and pass through a strainer into a cocktail glass. Serve with a dash of Lemon Peel Juice on top.

Using Peach or Orange Bitters makes a pleasant variation.

FLASH

1 teaspoon ANGOSTURA BITTERS
3 parts GIN
1 teaspoon PERNOD
1 CHERRY
1 dash of LEMON PEEL JUICE
½ shakerful of broken ICE

Half fill the shaker with broken Ice and add the Angostura Bitters. Then add the Gin and Pernod. Shake up and strain into a cocktail glass. Serve with a Cherry and a dash of Lemon Peel Juice.

Anisette may be used in place of Pernod, if desired. This makes a delightful variation.

FLORIDA

1 ½ parts ANGOSTURA BITTERS
The juice of ¼ LEMON
The juice of ¼ ORANGE
1 dash of PLAIN SYRUP
1 CHERRY
1 dash of LEMON PEEL JUICE
½ shakerful of broken ICE

Half fill the shaker with broken Ice and add the Angostura Bitters. Then put in the Lemon Juice, Orange Juice and Plain Syrup. Shake well and strain into a cocktail glass. Serve with a Cherry and a dash of Lemon Peel Juice on top.

GANGSTER

1 ½ parts BRANDY
1 ½ parts BROWN CURACAO
1 CHERRY
1 dash of LEMON PEEL JUICE
½ shakerful of broken ICE

Half fill the shaker with broken Ice. Then put in the Brandy and Brown Curaçao. Shake well and pass through a strainer into a cocktail glass. Serve with a Cherry and a dash of Lemon Peel Juice.

This is quite a strong cocktail and should not be drunk on an empty stomach.

GIBSON

1 ½ parts DRY GIN
1 ½ parts FRENCH VERMOUTH
1 small piece of GARLIC
½ tumblerful of broken ICE

The tumbler is half filled with broken Ice and the Dry Gin is added. Now put in the French Vermouth. Stir well. Smear the inside of a cocktail glass with the Garlic and then strain the mixture into it.

This is a dry cocktail. Be very sparing with the Garlic or the whole flavour of the cocktail will be masked.

GIN COCKTAIL

1 dash of ANGOSTURA BITTERS
2 dashes of BROWN CURACAO
2 parts GIN
1 CHERRY
1 dash of LEMON PEEL JUICE
½ tumblerful of broken ICE

Half fill a tumbler with broken Ice and add the Angostura Bitters. Then add the Brown Curaçao and Gin. Stir well and pass through a strainer into a cocktail glass. Serve with a Cherry and a dash of Lemon Peel Juice on top.

A cocktail of medium strength. Rum or Scotch may be used instead of the Gin.

GREAT GUNS

¾ part FRENCH VERMOUTH
1 part DUBONNET
¾ part PALE SHERRY
2 dashes of ANGOSTURA BITTERS
1 CHERRY
1 dash of LEMON PEEL JUICE
½ tumblerful of broken ICE

Half fill a tumbler with broken Ice and add the French Vermouth. Then add the Dubonnet, Sherry and Angostura Bitters. Stir well and pass through a strainer into a cocktail glass. Serve with a Cherry and a dash of Lemon Peel Juice on top.

This cocktail can be varied by using Orange Bitters and Orange Peel Juice instead of Angostura Bitters and Lemon Peel Juice, respectively.

HARRISON

2 parts GIN
½ teaspoon powdered SUGAR
1 part LEMON (or LIME) JUICE
1 teaspoon ANGOSTURA BITTERS
½ shakerful of broken ICE

The shaker is half filled with broken Ice and the Gin is added. Then put in the Sugar, Lemon (or Lime) Juice and Angostura Bitters. Shake well and pass through a strainer into a cocktail glass.

A medium strength cocktail, useful for serving at grown-up parties.

HARVARD

2 or 3 dashes of ANGOSTURA BITTERS
1 part ITALIAN VERMOUTH
½ teaspoon PLAIN SYRUP
1 part BRANDY
1 CHERRY
1 or 2 dashes of LEMON PEEL JUICE
½ tumblerful of broken ICE

*Half fill a tumbler with broken Ice and add the
Angostura Bitters. Then add the Italian Vermouth,
Plain Syrup and Brandy. Stir up and pass through
a strainer into a cocktail glass. Serve with a
Cherry and a dash of Lemon Peel Juice on top.*
    This cocktail is fairly strong.

HOLLYWOOD

¾ part FRENCH VERMOUTH
¾ part ITALIAN VERMOUTH
1 ½ parts DRY GIN
2 dashes of BROWN CURACAO
1 CHERRY
1 dash of LEMON PEEL JUICE
½ tumblerful of broken ICE

Half fill a tumbler with broken Ice and add the French Vermouth. Then put in the Italian Vermouth, Dry Gin and Brown Curaçao. Stir well and pass through a strainer into a cocktail glass. Serve with a Cherry and a dash of Lemon Peel Juice on top.

This cocktail is very popular in America. If required dry, double the quantity of French Vermouth and leave out the Italian.

IKA

1 part GRENADINE SYRUP
2 parts GIN
1 dash of LEMON PEEL JUICE
½ tumblerful of broken ICE

The tumbler is half filled with broken Ice and the Grenadine Syrup is added. Now add the Gin and stir well. Strain into a cocktail glass and serve with a dash of Lemon Peel Juice on top.

This is a very pleasant cocktail of medium strength.

INCA

1 teaspoon ORANGE BITTERS
¾ part GIN
¾ part FRENCH VERMOUTH
¾ part DRY SHERRY
1 teaspoon PLAIN SYRUP
1 CHERRY
1 dash of ORANGE PEEL JUICE
½ a tumblerful of broken ICE

The tumbler is ½ half filled with broken Ice and the Orange Bitters is added. Next add the Gin, French Vermouth, Dry Sherry and Plain Syrup. Stir well and pass through a strainer into a cocktail glass. Serve with a Cherry and a dash of Orange Peel Juice on top.

INDIAN

½ teaspoon ORANGE BITTERS
¾ part CANADIAN CLUB WHISKY
¾ part ITALIAN VERMOUTH
¾ part GIN
½ teaspoon TRIPLE SEC COINTREAU
½ teaspoon BROWN CURACAO
1 dash of LEMON PEEL JUICE
½ tumblerful of broken ICE

Half fill a tumbler with broken Ice and add the Orange Bitters. Then add the Canadian Club Whisky, Italian Vermouth, Gin, Cointreau and Brown Curaçao. Stir well and pass through a strainer into a cocktail glass. Serve with a dash of Lemon Peel Juice on top.

This is a fairly strong cocktail, not advised in hot weather.

JACK ROSE

1 part LEMON JUICE
1 teaspoon GRENADINE SYRUP
2 parts CALVADOS
1 or 2 dashes of LEMON PEEL JUICE
½ shakerful of broken ICE

The shaker is half filled with broken Ice and the Lemon Juice is added. Then add the Grenadine Syrup and Calvados. Shake well and pass through a strainer into a cocktail glass. Serve with a dash of Lemon Peel Juice on top.

Lime Juice may be substituted if desired. This makes a pleasant change.

J.J. MURPHY

1 ½ parts GIN
¾ part FRENCH VERMOUTH
¾ part ITALIAN VERMOUTH
1 dash of BENEDICTINE
1 CHERRY
1 dash of LEMON PEEL JUICE
½ tumblerful of broken ICE

Half fill a tumbler with broken Ice and add the Gin. Now add the French Vermouth, Italian Vermouth and Bénédictine. Stir well and pass through a strainer into a cocktail glass. Serve with a Cherry and a dash of Lemon Peel Juice.

A cocktail of medium strength.

KURSAAL

1 dash of ANGOSTURA BITTERS
1 dash of ORANGE BITTERS
1 ½ parts BRANDY
¾ part CHERRY BRANDY
¾ part FRENCH VERMOUTH
1 dash of PERNOD
1 teaspoon PLAIN SYRUP
1 CHERRY
1 dash of LEMON PEEL JUICE
½ shakerful of broken ICE

Half fill the shaker with broken Ice and add the Angostura Bitters. Then add the Orange Bitters, Brandy, Cherry Brandy, French Vermouth, Pernod and Plain Syrup. Shake well and pass through a strainer into a small wine glass. Serve with a Cherry and a dash of Lemon Peel Juice on top.

If you have no Cherry Brandy you can still make this cocktail by doubling the quantity of French Vermouth.

LIDO

1 ½ parts DRY GIN
1 ½ parts FRENCH VERMOUTH
2 dashes of APRICOT BRANDY
1 CHERRY
½ tumblerful of broken ICE

Half fill a tumbler with broken Ice and add the Gin. Then add the French Vermouth and Apricot Brandy. Stir well and pass through a strainer into a cocktail glass. Serve with a Cherry.

If you have no Apricot Brandy you can use Cherry Brandy instead.

LONDON

1 teaspoon ORANGE BITTERS
2 parts DRY GIN
1 teaspoon PERNOD
2 teaspoons PLAIN SYRUP
1 dash of ORANGE PEEL JUICE
½ tumblerful of broken ICE

Half fill a tumbler with broken Ice and add the Orange Bitters. Then add the Dry Gin, Pernod and Plain Syrup. Stir well and pass through a strainer into a cocktail glass. Serve with a dash of Orange Peel Juice on top.

If this is sweeter than desired, reduce the quantity of Plain Syrup.

LUIGI

1 ½ parts FRENCH VERMOUTH
A few drops of COINTREAU
1 ½ parts GIN
The juice of ½ ORANGE
2 or 3 dashes of GRENADINE
1 dash of ORANGE PEEL JUICE
½ shakerful of broken ICE

Half fill the shaker with broken Ice and add the French Vermouth. Then add the Cointreau, Gin, Orange Juice and Grenadine. Shake well and pass through a strainer into a cocktail glass. Serve with a dash of Orange Peel Juice on top.

Some people prefer to use Tangerine Juice and Tangerine Peel Juice in place of the Orange Juice and the Orange Peel Juice respectively. This makes a pleasant alternative.

MALIBU

1 teaspoon ANGOSTURA BITTERS
1 part FRENCH VERMOUTH
2 parts GIN
1 teaspoon PERNOD
1 dash of LEMON PEEL JUICE
1 OLIVE
½ tumblerful of broken ICE

Half fill a tumbler with broken Ice and add the Angostura Bitters. Then add the French Vermouth, Gin and Pernod. Stir well and pass through a strainer into a cocktail glass. Serve with a dash of Lemon Peel Juice on top and the Olive.

This cocktail is named after the famous coast resort near Hollywood. It is very refreshing in hot weather.

MANHATTAN 1

1 ½ parts CANADIAN CLUB WHISKY
1 ½ parts ITALIAN VERMOUTH
1 or 2 dashes of ANGOSTURA BITTERS
1 CHERRY
½ tumblerful of broken ICE

Half fill a tumbler with broken Ice and first add the Canadian Club Whisky, then Italian Vermouth and Angostura Bitters. Stir well and pass through a strainer into a cocktail glass. Serve with a Cherry.

One of the best-known cocktails: it deserves to be a favourite.

MANHATTAN 2

(Dry)
1 ½ parts CANADIAN CLUB WHISKY
1 ½ parts FRENCH VERMOUTH
1 or 2 dashes of ANGOSTURA BITTERS
1 CHERRY
½ tumblerful of broken ICE

This cocktail is prepares as in the previous recipe, but French Vermouth is used instead of Italian Vermouth. A much drier cocktail.

MANHATTAN 3

(Medium)
1 ½ parts CANADIAN CLUB WHISKY
¼ part ITALIAN VERMOUTH
¼ part FRENCH VERMOUTH
1 or 2 dashes of ANGOSTURA BITTERS
1 CHERRY
½ tumblerful of broken ICE

Make up as before, but in this case a blend of Italian and French Vermouth is used.

MANHATTAN 4

---

1 ½ parts CANADIAN CLUB WHISKY
1 ½ parts ITALIAN VERMOUTH
1 dash of ANGOSTURA BITTERS
1 dash of PERNOD
2 dashes of BROWN CURACAO
1 small piece of ORANGE or LEMON
   PEEL
1 CHERRY
½ tumblerful of broken ICE

Make up as before and serve with a piece of Orange or Lemon Peel on top. This cocktail has a lot more 'kick' in it than the others.

MARTINEZ 1

(Sweet)
1 or 2 dashes of ANGOSTURA BITTERS
1 ½ parts ITALIAN VERMOUTH
1 ½ parts GIN
1 CHERRY or OLIVE
1 dash of LEMON PEEL JUICE
½ tumblerful of broken ICE

Half fill a tumbler with broken Ice and add the Angostura Bitters. Then add the Italian Vermouth and Gin. Stir well and pass through a strainer into a cocktail glass. Serve with a Cherry or an Olive and a dash of Lemon Peel Juice on top. Very popular.

MARTINEZ 2

(Medium)
¾ part FRENCH VERMOUTH
¾ part ITALIAN VERMOUTH
1 ½ parts GIN
1 or 2 dashes of ANGOSTURA BITTERS
1 dash of LEMON PEEL JUICE
1 CHERRY or OLIVE
½ tumblerful of broken ICE

This cocktail is made up in exactly the same way as the previous one, except that both French Vermouth and Italian Vermouth are used instead of only Italian.

MARTINEZ 3

(Dry)
1 ½ parts FRENCH VERMOUTH
1 ½ parts GIN
1 or 2 dashes of ANGOSTURA BITTERS
1 dash of LEMON PEEL JUICE
1 CHERRY or OLIVE
½ tumblerful of broken ICE

This cocktail is made up in exactly the same way as the Sweet Martinez cocktail: but French Vermouth is used instead of Italian Vermouth.

MARTINEZ SPECIAL

1 part FRENCH VERMOUTH
1 ½ parts GIN
1 ½ teaspoons MARASCHINO
1 teaspoon ORANGE BITTERS
¼ teaspoon ANGOSTURA BITTERS
1 dash of ORANGE PEEL JUICE
1 CHERRY or OLIVE
½ shakerful of broken ICE

This cocktail is made up in exactly the same way as the previous cocktail except that the Maraschino and the Orange Bitters are added, and also, it is served with a dash of Orange Peel Juice instead of Lemon.

MARTINI 1

(Sweet)
2 parts DRY GIN
1 part ITALIAN VERMOUTH
    (MARTINI'S)
½ teaspoon ORANGE BITTERS
1 or 2 dashes of LEMON PEEL JUICE
½ tumblerful of broken ICE

Half fill a tumbler with broken Ice and add the Dry Gin. Then add the Italian Vermouth and Orange Bitters. Stir well and pass through a strainer into a cocktail glass. Squeeze 1 or 2 dashes of Lemon Peel Juice on top.

    This is the original recipe and it has never been improved upon.

MARTINI 2

(Medium)
¾ part FRENCH VERMOUTH
¾ part ITALIAN VERMOUTH
1 ½ parts DRY GIN
1 or 2 dashes of LEMON PEEL JUICE
½ tumblerful of broken ICE

Make up as before, but in this case a blend of both Italian Vermouth and French Vermouth is used.

MARTINI 3

(Dry)
1 ½ parts DRY GIN
1 ½ parts FRENCH VERMOUTH
1 dash of LEMON PEEL JUICE
½ tumblerful of broken ICE

Make up in exactly the same way as the Sweet Martini cocktail; but use French Vermouth instead of Italian Vermouth.

MARTINI SPECIAL

1 teaspoon RASPBERRY SYRUP
¾ part ITALIAN VERMOUTH
1 ½ parts DRY GIN
½ teaspoon PERNOD
½ teaspoon MARASCHINO
1 dash of LEMON PEEL JUICE
½ shakerful of broken ICE

The shaker is half filled with broken Ice and the Raspberry Syrup is added. Then add the Italian Vermouth, Dry Gin, Pernod and Maraschino. Shake up and pass through a strainer into a cocktail glass. Serve with a dash of Lemon Peel Juice.

This makes a pleasant variation from the ordinary Martini cocktails.

MIAMI

1 ½ parts PALE SHERRY
1 teaspoon ORANGE BITTERS
1 ½ parts DUBONNET
1 CHERRY
1 dash of ORANGE PEEL JUICE
½ tumblerful of broken ICE

Half fill a tumbler with broken Ice and add the Pale Sherry. Then put in the Orange Bitters and Dubonnet. Stir up and pass through a strainer into a cocktail glass. Serve with a Cherry and a dash of Orange Peel Juice on top.

A very refreshing cocktail.

MILLIONAIRE

1 dash of ORANGE BITTERS
2 parts CANADIAN CLUB WHISKY
1 teaspoon BROWN CURACAO
1 dash of PERNOD
1 teaspoon GRENADINE SYRUP
The white of a fresh EGG
1 CHERRY
½ shakerful of broken ICE

Half fill the shaker with broken Ice and add the Orange Bitters. Then put in the Canadian Club Whisky, Brown Curaçao, Pernod, Grenadine Syrup and Egg White. Shake well and pass through a strainer into a cocktail glass. Serve with a Cherry.

The Pernod improves the flavour of this cocktail, but it can be omitted if desired.

MONKEY GLAND

6 or 7 dashes of GRENADINE SYRUP
4 or 5 dashes of PERNOD
2 parts GIN
2 parts ORANGE JUICE
1 dash of ORANGE PEEL JUICE
½ shakerful of broken ICE

The shaker is half filled with broken Ice and the Grenadine Syrup added. Then add the Pernod, Gin and Orange Juice. Shake well and pass through a strainer into a wine glass. Serve with a dash of Orange Peel Juice on top.

Raspberry Syrup may be used instead of Grenadine Syrup, if desired. Both are rather sweet and some may prefer to reduce the quantity of the Syrup.

MONTSERRAT

2 parts DRY GIN
2 teaspoons LIME JUICE
1 teaspoon GRENADINE SYRUP
2 dashes of PERNOD
1 CHERRY
½ shakerful of broken ICE

Half fill the shaker with broken Ice and add the Dry Gin. Then add the Lime Juice, Grenadine Syrup and Pernod. Shake well and pass through a strainer into a cocktail glass. Serve with a Cherry.

This cocktail is very refreshing and is of medium strength.

MORNING

1 teaspoon ANGOSTURA BITTERS
1 teaspoon PERNOD
2 parts BRANDY
2 parts ITALIAN VERMOUTH
1 teaspoon MARASCHINO
1 CHERRY
1 slice of LEMON
½ tumblerful of broken ICE

Half fill a tumbler with broken Ice and add the Angostura Bitters. Then put in the Pernod, Brandy, Italian Vermouth and Maraschino. Stir well and strain into a wine glass. Serve with a Cherry and a slice of Lemon.

This recipe can be varied by reducing, the quantity of Maraschino by half and adding ½ teaspoon Brown Curaçao.

MURMURER

½ teaspoon ANGOSTURA BITTERS
1 ½ parts GIN
1 ½ parts SHERRY
¼ teaspoon LIME JUICE
1 dash of LEMON PEEL JUICE
½ tumblerful of broken ICE

Half fill a tumbler with broken Ice and add the Angostura Bitters. Then add the Gin, Sherry and Lime Juice. Stir well and pass through a strainer into a cocktail glass. Serve with a dash of Lemon Peel Juice on top.

This is a very pleasant cocktail of medium strength.

OLD-FASHIONED

1 lump of LOAF SUGAR
1 ½ teaspoons WATER
1 teaspoon ORANGE BITTERS
1 teaspoon ANGOSTURA BITTERS
3 parts BENEDICTINE
1 dash of LEMON PEEL JUICE
1 small lump of ICE

This cocktail is prepared and served in a large wine glass. Put the lump of Sugar in the wine glass and add the Water. Then crush the Sugar with a spoon and add the lump of Ice, the Orange Bitters, Angostura Bitters and Bénédictine. Stir well and serve with a dash of Lemon Peel Juice on top.

Any other liqueur can be used in place of the Bénédictine, if desired.

OLIVETTE

2 dashes of ORANGE BITTERS
2 dashes of ANGOSTURA BITTERS
2 dashes of PLAIN SYRUP
1 ½ parts FRENCH VERMOUTH
1 ½ parts DRY GIN
2 dashes of PERNOD
1 OLIVE
2 dashes of LEMON PEEL JUICE
½ tumblerful of broken ICE

Half fill a tumbler with broken Ice and add the Orange Bitters. Then add the Angostura Bitters, Plain Syrup, French Vermouth, Dry Gin and Pernod. Stir well and pass through a strainer into a small wine glass. Serve with an Olive and a dash of Lemon Peel Juice on top.

If preferred, Italian Vermouth can be used instead of French.

ORANGE BLOSSOM

A few drops of ORANGE BITTERS
1 ½ parts DRY GIN
½ teaspoon GRENADINE SYRUP
1 ½ parts ORANGE SQUASH
1 dash of ORANGE PEEL JUICE
½ shakerful of broken ICE

Half fill the shaker with broken Ice and add the Orange Bitters. Then add the Dry Gin, Grenadine Syrup and Orange Squash. Shake well and strain into a cocktail glass. Serve with a dash of Orange Peel Juice on top.

If this is sweeter than required, reduce the quantity of Grenadine Syrup.

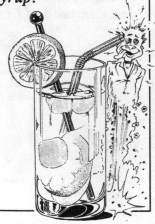

PARADISE

¾ part DRY GIN
¾ part LEMON SQUASH
1 ½ parts APRICOT BRANDY
1 slice of LEMON
1 dash of LEMON PEEL JUICE
1 shakerful of broken ICE

Half fill the shaker with broken Ice and add the Dry Gin. Then add the Lemon Squash and Apricot Brandy. Shake well and pass through a strainer into a cocktail glass. Serve with a slice of lemon and a dash of Lemon Peel Juice on top.

This recipe can be varied by using Orange Juice, Tangerine Juice or Grapefruit Juice instead of Lemon Squash. All are excellent.

PERFECT

1 part ITALIAN VERMOUTH
1 part FRENCH VERMOUTH
3 parts DRY GIN
2 dashes of PERNOD
1 slice of LEMON
1 dash of LEMON PEEL JUICE
½ shakerful of broken ICE

Half fill the shaker with broken Ice and add the Italian Vermouth. Then put in the French Vermouth, Dry Gin and Pernod. Shake well and pass through a strainer into a wine glass. Serve with a slice of Lemon and a dash of Lemon Peel Juice on top.

This cocktail is pleasant and fairly strong.

PING PONG

1 dash of ANGOSTURA BITTERS
1 ½ parts SLOE GIN
1 ½ parts ITALIAN VERMOUTH
1 CHERRY
½ tumblerful of broken ICE

Half fill a tumbler with broken Ice and add the Angostura Bitters. Then add the Sloe Gin and Italian Vermouth. Stir well and pass through a strainer into a cocktail glass. Serve with a Cherry.

Another way of making up this cocktail is to use French Vermouth in place of Italian.

PINA COLADA

2 parts WHITE RUM or TEQUILA
2 parts COCONUT CREAM
3 parts PINEAPPLE JUICE
1 MARASCHINO CHERRY

Blend the ingredients in a blender or shake vigorously. Pour into a tall glass and garnish with a cherry or a piece of pineapple.

RIALTO

2 sprigs of MINT
2 lumps of SUGAR
2 dashes of ORANGE BITTERS
1 ½ parts ITALIAN VERMOUTH
1 dash of ORANGE SQUASH
1 ½ parts CALVADOS
1 slice of ORANGE
½ tumblerful of broken ICE

Half fill a tumbler with broken Ice and add 1 sprig of Mint. Then, add the Sugar, Orange Bitters, Italian Vermouth, Orange Squash and Calvados. Stir well and pass through a strainer into a cocktail glass. Serve with a slice of Orange and a sprig of Mint.

This is a delightful cocktail, fairly strong.

RIVIERA

3 or 4 dashes of LEMON SQUASH
1 dash of GRENADINE SYRUP
3 parts DRY GIN
1 ½ parts CALVADOS
1 slice of LEMON
½ shakerful of broken ICE

The shaker is half filled with broken Ice and the Lemon Squash is added. Then add the Grenadine Syrup, Dry Gin and Calvados. Shake well and pass through a strainer into a small wine glass. Serve with a slice of Lemon.

This cocktail is very popular in Paris and on the Riviera.

ROB ROY

1 dash of ORANGE BITTERS
2 dashes of ANGOSTURA BITTERS
1 part FRENCH VERMOUTH
1 part SCOTCH WHISKY
2 dashes of BROWN CURACAO
1 CHERRY
2 dashes of LEMON PEEL JUICE
½ tumblerful of broken ICE

Half fill a tumbler with broken Ice and add the Orange Bitters. Then add the Angostura Bitters, French Vermouth, Scotch Whisky and Brown Curaçao. Stir well and pass through a strainer into a cocktail glass. Serve with a Cherry and a dash of Lemon Peel Juice on top.

The Curaçao can be omitted, if desired. Another variation is to use Italian Vermouth in place of French.

ROSE

1 part FRENCH VERMOUTH
1 teaspoon GRENADINE SYRUP
1 part ORANGE JUICE
1 part DRY GIN
1 CHERRY
1 dash of ORANGE PEEL JUICE
½ shakerful of broken ICE

Half fill the shaker with broken Ice and add the French Vermouth. Then, add the Grenadine Syrup, Orange Juice and Dry Gin. Shake well and pass through a strainer into a cocktail glass. Serve with a Cherry and a dash of Orange Peel Juice on top.

Some people prefer to add a dash of Dubonnet. This improves the cocktail, in the opinion of some connoisseurs.

ROYAL

2 dashes of ORANGE BITTERS
1 ½ parts DUBONNET
3 parts GIN
1 CHERRY
1 or 2 dashes of ORANGE PEEL JUICE
½ tumblerful of broken ICE

The tumbler is half filled with broken Ice and the Orange Bitters added. Then, add the Dubonnet and Gin. Stir well and pass through a strainer into a small wine glass. Serve with a Cherry and a dash of Orange Peel Juice on top.

This cocktail makes an excellent aperitif.

ROYAL CLOVER

3 parts DRY GIN
1 teaspoon GRENADINE SYRUP
The juice of a LEMON
The yolk of an EGG
1 dash of grated NUTMEG
½ shakerful of broken ICE

This cocktail is prepared in exactly the same way as the Clover Club Cocktail 2 on page 35, except that the yolk is used instead of the white of an Egg.

If preferred, half of the quantity of Dry Gin may be used and ¼ part of French Vermouth added.

SHERRY

---

2 parts SHERRY
2 dashes of ANGOSTURA BITTERS
2 dashes of ORANGE BITTERS
1 dash of ORANGE PEEL JUICE
1 CHERRY
½ tumblerful of broken ICE

This cocktail is made up in exactly the same way as the Gin Cocktail on page 55, except that Sherry and Orange Bitters are used instead of Gin and Brown Curaçao.

SIDECAR 1

The juice of ¼ LEMON
1 ½ parts BRANDY
¾ part DRY GIN
½ shakerful of broken ICE

Half fill the shaker with broken Ice and squeeze in the juice of ¼ Lemon. Then add the Brandy and Dry Gin. Shake well and pass through a strainer into a cocktail glass.

This is a great favourite among the French and is fairly strong.

SIDECAR 2

The juice of ¼ LEMON
1 ½ parts BRANDY
¼ part COINTREAU
½ shakerful of broken ICE

This cocktail is made up in exactly the same way as the previous one except that Cointreau is used instead of Dry Gin.

SILVER

1 teaspoon ORANGE BITTERS
2 parts DRY GIN
1 part ITALIAN VERMOUTH
1 teaspoon MARASCHINO
1 CHERRY
1 dash of LEMON PEEL JUICE
½ shakerful of broken ICE

The shaker is half filled with broken Ice and the Orange Bitters added. Then add the Dry Gin, Italian Vermouth and Maraschino. Shake well and strain into a cocktail glass. Serve with a Cherry and a dash of Lemon Peel Juice on top. A cocktail of medium strength.

STAR

2 dashes of ORANGE BITTERS
1 ½ parts CALVADOS
1 ½ parts ITALIAN VERMOUTH
1 teaspoon BROWN CURACAO
1 slice of LEMON
1 dash of LEMON PEEL JUICE
½ tumblerful of broken ICE

Half fill a tumbler with broken Ice and add the Orange Bitters. Then add the Calvados, Italian Vermouth and Brown Curaçao. Stir well and pass through a strainer into a cocktail glass. Serve with a slice of Lemon and a dash of Lemon Peel Juice on top.

This cocktail is sometimes served with an Olive in place of the slice of Lemon.

SUNSHINE

1 teaspoon ORANGE BITTERS
¾ part ITALIAN VERMOUTH
1 ½ parts GIN
1 ½ parts ORANGE SQUASH
1 teaspoon GRENADINE SYRUP
1 CHERRY
½ tumblerful of broken ICE

The tumbler is half filled with the broken Ice and the Orange Bitters added. Then add the Italian Vermouth, Gin, Orange Squash and Grenadine Syrup. Stir well and pass through a strainer into a small wine glass. Serve with a Cherry.

This is a very pleasant cocktail of medium strength.

TOP NOTCH

1 ½ parts FRENCH VERMOUTH
1 ½ parts SLOE GIN
1 teaspoon RASPBERRY SYRUP
1 CHERRY
½ shakerful of broken ICE

Half fill the shaker with broken Ice. Then put in the French Vermouth, Sloe Gin and Raspberry Syrup. Shake well and pass through a strainer into a cocktail glass. Serve with a Cherry.

This is a sweet cocktail and is very popular among the fair sex.

TORONTO

1 ½ parts DRY GIN
¾ part SCOTCH WHISKY
3 parts DUBONNET
1 CHERRY
1 dash of LEMON PEEL JUICE
½ tumblerful of broken ICE

The tumbler is half filled with broken Ice and the Dry Gin added. Then add the Scotch Whisky and Dubonnet. Stir well and pass through a strainer into a cocktail glass. Serve with a Cherry and a dash of Lemon Peel Juice on top.

An excellent aperitif.

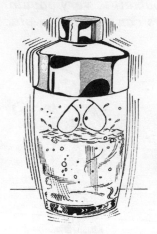

TURF

1 teaspoon **ORANGE BITTERS**
2 parts **DRY GIN**
1 part **FRENCH VERMOUTH**
1 teaspoon **PERNOD**
1 teaspoon **MARASCHINO**
1 **OLIVE**
½ tumblerful of broken **ICE**

Half fill a tumbler with broken Ice and add the Orange Bitters. Then add the Dry Gin, French Vermouth, Pernod and Maraschino. Stir well and pass through a strainer into a cocktail glass. Serve with an Olive.

This cocktail is very popular. If desired Peach Bitters can be used in place of Orange Bitters.

TUXEDO

1 teaspoon ANGOSTURA BITTERS
1 part ITALIAN VERMOUTH
2 parts GIN
1 teaspoon MARASCHINO
2 dashes of PERNOD
1 CHERRY
1 dash of LEMON PEEL JUICE
½ tumblerful of broken ICE

*The tumbler is half filled with broken Ice and the
Angostura Bitters added. Then add the Italian
Vermouth, Gin, Maraschino and Pernod. Stir well
and pass through a strainer into a small wine glass.
Serve with a Cherry and a dash of Lemon Peel
Juice on top.*

This is a very popular cocktail.

WHISKY

2 parts SCOTCH WHISKY
1 dash of ANGOSTURA BITTERS
2 dashes of BROWN CURACAO
1 dash of LEMON PEEL JUICE
1 CHERRY
1 lump of SUGAR
½ tumblerful of broken ICE

*Make up in exactly the same way as for Gin
Cocktail on page 55, but use the altered
ingredients.*

WONDER BAR

½ teaspoon ANGOSTURA BITTERS
½ teaspoon ORANGE BITTERS
¾ part ITALIAN VERMOUTH
¾ part FRENCH VERMOUTH
2 parts DRY GIN
1 CHERRY
1 dash of LEMON PEEL JUICE
½ tumblerful of broken ICE

Half fill a tumbler with broken Ice and add the Angostura Bitters. Then add the Orange Bitters, Italian Vermouth, French Vermouth and Dry Gin. Stir well and pass through a strainer into a small wine glass. Serve with a Cherry and a dash of Lemon Peel Juice on top.

This is a rather pleasant and fairly strong cocktail.

YOKOHAMA

1 part GIN
1 part ITALIAN VERMOUTH
1 part CREME DE MENTHE
1 OLIVE
1 dash of LEMON PEEL JUICE
½ shakerful of broken ICE

Half fill the shaker with broken Ice and add the Gin. Then add the Italian Vermouth and Crème de Menthe. Shake well and pass through a strainer into a cocktail glass. Serve with an Olive and a dash of Lemon Peel Juice on top.

If required not quite so sweet, use French Vermouth in place of Italian.

YORK

1 dash of ORANGE BITTERS
1 dash of ANGOSTURA BITTERS
1 ½ parts ITALIAN VERMOUTH
1 ½ parts SCOTCH WHISKY
1 dash of LEMON PEEL JUICE
½ tumblerful of broken ICE

Half fill a tumbler with broken Ice and add the Orange Bitters. Then add the Angostura Bitters, Italian Vermouth and Scotch Whisky. Stir well and pass through a strainer into a cocktail glass. Serve with a dash of Lemon Peel Juice on top.

If you prefer the dry type of cocktail, you can use French Vermouth in place of Italian.

ZA ZA

---

2 dashes of ANGOSTURA BITTERS
1 ½ parts DRY GIN
1 ½ parts DUBONNET
½ shakerful of broken ICE

Half fill the shaker with broken Ice and add the Angostura Bitters. Then add the Dry Gin and Dubonnet. Shake well and pass through a strainer into a cocktail glass.

This cocktail is an excellent aperitif.

ZERO HOUR

---

1 ½ parts BRANDY
¾ part APRICOT BRANDY
3 dashes of CREME DE MENTHE
1 OLIVE
2 dashes of PERNOD
½ shakerful of broken ICE

The shaker is half filled with broken Ice and the Brandy added. Then the Apricot Brandy and Crème de Menthe are added. Shake well and pass through a strainer into a cocktail glass. Serve with an Olive and two dashes of Pernod on top.

FRUIT COCKTAILS

Mostly non-alcoholic

CIDER

1 dash of ANGOSTURA BITTERS
½ teaspoon PLAIN SYRUP
4 ½ parts CIDER
1 slice of LEMON
½ tumblerful of broken ICE

Half fill a tumbler with broken Ice and add the Angostura Bitters. Then add the Plain Syrup and Cider. Stir well and pass through a strainer into a small wine glass. Serve with a slice of Lemon on top.

Use non- alcoholic Cider if desired.

GRAPE

1 dash of ANGOSTURA BITTERS
1 ½ parts GRAPE JUICE
3 parts PLAIN SYRUP
6 parts SODA WATER
2 slices of FRESH FRUIT
½ tumblerful of broken ICE

Half fill a tumbler with broken Ice and add the Angostura Bitters. Then add the Grape Juice and Plain Syrup. Stir well and pass through a strainer into a tumbler. Fill up with Soda Water. Serve with slices of Fresh Fruit on top.

A delightful drink in hot weather, and one that contains a good deal of vitamins.

GRAPEFRUIT

1 GRAPEFRUIT
2 BANANAS
1 small tin of PINEAPPLE CHUNKS
CASTOR SUGAR
6 parts SHERRY
STRAWBERRIES OR GLACE FRUITS
ICE CHIPS

Remove the peel, pulp and pips from the Grapefruit and press it through a sieve. Slice the Bananas and Pineapple thinly; add them to the Grapefruit purée, in equal quantities, making 600ml (1 pint) altogether. Sprinkle Castor Sugar on the fruit and pour the Sherry over it. Stand on Ice for about an hour. Serve in sherbet glasses and decorate with fresh Strawberries or Glacé Fruits.

MINT

1 dash of ANGOSTURA BITTERS
3 parts CREME DE MENTHE
3 parts LIME JUICE
4 ½ parts SODA WATER
2 sprigs of MINT
Slices of FRESH FRUIT
½ tumblerful of broken ICE

Half fill a tumbler with broken Ice and add the Angostura Bitters. Then add the Crème de Menthe and Lime Juice. Stir well and pass through a strainer into a tumbler. Fill up with Soda Water. Serve with Mint sprigs and slices of Fresh Fruit on top.

If desired, you can alter the flavour of this cocktail by using Peppermint in place of Crème de Menthe.

MIXED FRUIT

1 ORANGE
½ GRAPEFRUIT
1 BANANA
1 cup GRAPES with the seeds removed
7 or 8 CHERRIES
3 dashes of MARASCHINO (or
    PINEAPPLE SYRUP)
2 teaspoons powdered SUGAR

Peel the Orange and the half of a Grapefruit, separate into sections and put into a large sundae glass. Then add the Banana (cut into slices), Grapes and Cherries. Pour over the top 3 dashes of Maraschino or Pineapple Syrup and sprinkle with Sugar.

ORANGES AND LEMONS

1 ORANGE
1 LEMON
2 or 3 CHERRIES
1 dash of PEPPERMINT
2 teaspoons powdered SUGAR

Peel the Orange and Lemon, separate into sections and place in a sundae glass. Put the Cherries in the centre of the glass and add the dash of Peppermint. Serve with the Sugar on top.

This recipe is very popular because it can be prepared so easily with ingredients that are present in many households.

RASPBERRY SMASH

1 dash of ANGOSTURA BITTERS
1 ½ parts RASPBERRY JUICE AND
    PULP
1 ½ parts LEMON JUICE
A few RASPBERRIES
7 ½ parts SODA WATER
½ tumblerful of broken ICE

This fruit cocktail is prepared in exactly the same way as Grape Cocktail on page 113, except that Raspberry Juice and Pulp is used in place of Grape Juice. Serve with a few Raspberries on top instead of slices of Lemon and Fresh Fruit. If preferred, Loganberries or Blackberries may be used in place of Raspberries.

REFRESHER

STRAWBERRIES or similar fruit in
    season
LEMON JUICE
WATER
½ shakerful of broken ICE

Take a small quantity of Strawberries, Currants,
Raspberries or similar fruit in season. Squeeze out
the juice and strain into a shaker half full of broken
Ice. Pour in half as much Lemon Juice as fruit
juice and add a little Water. Shake well and strain
into a tumbler.

SUN DEW

1 dash of ANGOSTURA BITTERS
3 parts ORANGE JUICE
1 ½ parts PLAIN SYRUP
1 ½ parts GRAPE JUICE
4 ½ parts SODA WATER
2 slices of ORANGE
½ tumblerful of broken ICE

Half fill a tumbler with broken Ice and add the Angostura Bitters. Then put in the Orange Juice, Plain Syrup and Grape Juice. Stir well and pass through a strainer into a tumbler. Fill up with Soda Water. Serve with slices of Orange on top.
    A delightful drink - very refreshing.

OTHER DRINKS

*These are not true cocktails
but very much like them*

PERNOD COOLER

2 dashes of ANGOSTURA BITTERS
3 parts WHISKY
¾ part LEMON JUICE
300ml (½ pint) GINGER ALE
2 or 3 dashes of PERNOD
1 lump of ICE

*Put the lump of Ice in a tall glass and add the
Angostura Bitters. Then add the Whisky, Lemon
Juice and Ginger Ale. Stir well. Serve with two or
three dashes of Pernod on top.*
  A pleasant drink.

ANGEL'S KISS

1 ½ parts BENEDICTINE
1 ½ parts CREAM

*Use a cocktail glass. Put the Bénédictine into the
cocktail glass. Then put in the cream; do not stir.*
  A very popular drink.

ANGOSTURA FIZZ

¾ part PLAIN SYRUP
1 ½ parts ANGOSTURA BITTERS
3 parts LEMON JUICE
The white of an EGG
SODA WATER
½ shakerful of broken ICE

Half fill the shaker with broken Ice and add the Plain Syrup. Then add the Angostura Bitters, Lemon Juice and the white of an Egg. Shake well and pass through a strainer into a tumbler. To serve, fill up with Soda Water.

BACARDI CRUSTA

2 parts BACARDI
1 part LEMON JUICE
1 teaspoon PLAIN SYRUP
1 teaspoon PERNOD
2 dashes of ANGOSTURA BITTERS
The peel of a LEMON cut in a spiral
Slices of FRESH FRUIT
½ teaspoon powdered SUGAR
½ shakerful of broken ICE

This drink is prepared in exactly the same way as the Brandy Crusta on page 127, except that Bacardi is used in place of Brandy. Also the Orange Bitters is left out and double the quantity of Angostura Bitters is used.

Some people prefer to use Maraschino in place of Pernod.

BADMINTON CUP

1 bottle of CLARET
75g (3oz) ICING SUGAR
The juice and rind of 1 LEMON
4 ½ parts BROWN CURACAO
2 bottles of SODA WATER
3 slices of CUCUMBER
ICE CHIPS

Put the Claret into a large bowl and add the Sugar. Then add the Lemon Juice and Brown Curaçao. Stir well. Surround the bowl with the Ice and leave for half-an-hour; then strain the mixture and add the Soda Water. Serve in a large tumbler with the Lemon rind and the slices of Cucumber on top.

BRANDY COBBLER

6 parts BRANDY
1 ½ parts BROWN CURACAO
1 dash of LEMON PEEL JUICE
2 slices of LEMON
¼ tumblerful of broken ICE
½ shakerful of broken ICE

This is prepared in exactly the same way as Whisky Cobbler on page 156. Use Brandy instead of Whisky.

A very refreshing drink.

BRANDY CRUSTA

1 dash of ORANGE BITTERS
1 dash of ANGOSTURA BITTERS
1 part LEMON JUICE
1 teaspoon PLAIN SYRUP
2 parts BRANDY
1 teaspoon MARASCHINO
½ teaspoon powdered SUGAR
The peel of a LEMON cut in a spiral
Slices of FRESH FRUIT
½ shakerful of broken ICE

Half fill the shaker with broken Ice and add the Orange Bitters. Then add the Angostura Bitters, Lemon Juice, Plain Syrup, Brandy and Maraschino. Shake well and strain. Now moisten the inside of a wine glass with Lemon Juice and dip or sprinkle with Sugar. Then put in the Lemon peel, cut spiral fashion, and add the mixture. Serve with slices of Fresh Fruit.

BRANDY DAISY

3 parts BRANDY
3 parts LIME JUICE
3 parts LEMON JUICE
1 ½ parts GRENADINE SYRUP
SODA WATER
Slices of FRESH FRUIT
½ shakerful of broken ICE

Half fill the shaker with broken Ice and add the Brandy. Then put in the Lime Juice, Lemon Juice and Grenadine Syrup. Shake well, pass through a strainer into a large tumbler and fill up with Soda Water. Serve with slices of Fresh Fruit on top and with a spoon.

If you prefer it, you can halve the quantities of the above ingredients and serve in a large wine glass without adding the Soda Water.

BRANDY EGG NOGG

2 parts RUM
3 parts BRANDY
1 teaspoon SUGAR
1 EGG
1 dash of grated NUTMEG
4 ½ parts MILK
½ shakerful of broken ICE

Prepare in exactly the same way as for Egg Nogg on page 138.

This recipe is much stronger than the Egg Nogg recipe, owing to the larger quantity of Rum used.

BRANDY FIZZ

4 ½ parts LEMON JUICE
¾ part GRENADINE SYRUP
The white of an EGG
3 parts BRANDY
1 teaspoon BROWN CURACAO
SODA WATER
½ shakerful of broken ICE

Half fill the shaker with broken Ice and add the Lemon Juice. Then add the Grenadine Syrup, white of an Egg, Brandy and Brown Curaçao. Shake well and pass through a strainer into a tumbler. To serve, fill up the tumbler with Soda Water.

This drink is very pleasant and a very good pick-me-up.

BULLDOG COOLER

3 parts DRY GIN
The juice of ½ ORANGE
1 or 2 dashes of PLAIN SYRUP
200ml (⅓ pint) GINGER ALE
1 or 2 dashes of ORANGE PEEL JUICE
1 lump of ICE

Put the lump of Ice in a tall glass. Then add the Dry Gin, Orange Juice, Plain Syrup and Ginger Ale. Stir well and serve with a dash of Orange Peel Juice on top.

If this is sweeter than required, reduce the quantity of Plain Syrup.

BURGUNDY CUP

1 bottle of BURGUNDY
3 parts BRANDY
3 parts MARASCHINO
1 ½ parts BROWN CURACAO
2 or 3 dashes of BENEDICTINE
1 bottle of SODA WATER
2 or 3 slices of LEMON
1 or 2 slices of ORANGE
Slices of FRESH FRUIT
1 big lump of ICE

Put the piece of Ice into a large bowl and add the Burgundy. Then put in the Brandy, Maraschino, Brown Curaçao, Bénédictine and Soda Water. Stir well and strain the mixture. Serve in a large tumbler with the slices of Lemon, Orange and the Fresh Fruit on top.

CHAMPAGNE COBBLER

6 parts CHAMPAGNE
2 dashes of OLD BRANDY
3 or 4 dashes of PLAIN SYRUP
1 or 2 dashes of LEMON JUICE
1 dash of LEMON PEEL JUICE
2 slices of LEMON
½ bar-glassful of broken ICE
½ tumblerful of broken ICE

This drink is prepared in exactly the same way as the Moselle Cobbler on page 144, except that Champagne is used instead of Moselle.

A very refreshing drink.

CHAMPAGNE CUP

1 bottle of CHAMPAGNE
3 parts BRANDY
2 parts YELLOW CHARTREUSE
1 ½ parts MARASCHINO
1 ½ parts PLAIN SYRUP
1 bottle of SODA WATER
3 slices of LEMON
3 slices of ORANGE
3 slices of CUCUMBER
2 or 3 sprigs of MINT
Slices of FRESH FRUIT
1 big lump of ICE

Put the lump of Ice into a large bowl and add the Champagne. Then put in the Brandy, Yellow Chartreuse, Maraschino, Plain Syrup and Soda Water. Stir well and strain the mixture. Serve in a large tumbler with the slices of Lemon, Orange, Cucumber, sprigs of Mint and the Fresh Fruit on top.

Some people prefer to use Brown Curaçao in place of Yellow Chartreuse.

CIDER CUP

1 large bottle of CIDER
2 parts BROWN CURACAO
1 ½ parts MARASCHINO
3 parts BRANDY
4 ½ parts PALE SHERRY
1 teaspoon LEMON JUICE
2 or 3 slices of LEMON
2 or 3 slices of ORANGE
Slices of FRESH FRUIT
2 sprigs of MINT
1 big lump of ICE

Put the piece of Ice into a large bowl and add the Cider. Then put in the Brown Curaçao, Maraschino, Brandy, Pale Sherry and Lemon Juice. Stir well and strain the mixture. Serve in a large tumbler with the slices of Lemon, Orange, Fresh Fruit and the sprigs of Mint on top.

CLARET CUP

1.1 litres (2 pints) CLARET
1 ½ parts LEMON JUICE
3 parts BRANDY
2 parts BROWN CURACAO
1 ½ parts MARASCHINO
1 ½ parts PLAIN SYRUP
3 slices of LEMON
2 slices of ORANGE
1 slice of CUCUMBER
Slices of FRESH FRUIT
1 bottle of SODA WATER
1 big lump of ICE

Make up in exactly the same way as Champagne Cup on page 134 but use Claret in place of Champagne. Also add the Lemon Juice.

This cup is very popular indeed.

CLUB COOLER

2 parts ITALIAN VERMOUTH
1 dash of LEMON JUICE
1 part GRENADINE SYRUP
300ml (½ pint) SODA WATER
1 dash of LEMON PEEL JUICE
1 lump of ICE

Put the lump of Ice in a tall glass. Then add the Italian Vermouth, Lemon Juice, Grenadine Syrup and Soda Water. Stir well and serve with a dash of Lemon Peel Juice on top.

A very popular drink.

EGG NOGG

1 teaspoon SUGAR
1 EGG
1 dash of RUM
4 parts BRANDY
4 ½ parts MILK
1 dash of grated NUTMEG
½ shakerful of broken ICE

Half fill the shaker with broken Ice and add the Sugar. Then add the Egg, Rum, Brandy and Milk. Shake well and pass through a strainer into a tumbler. Serve with a dash of Nutmeg on top.

This recipe can be varied by using Gin, Rum or Whisky, in place of Brandy.

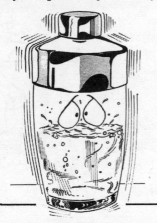

GIN CRUSTA

2 parts GIN
1 part LEMON JUICE
1 teaspoon PLAIN SYRUP
1 teaspoon MARASCHINO
1 dash of ORANGE BITTERS
1 dash of ANGOSTURA BITTERS
The peel of a LEMON cut spiral fashion
Slices of FRUIT
1 teaspoon powdered SUGAR
½ shakerful of broken ICE

Prepare in exactly the same way as for Brandy Crusta on page 127, but use Gin instead of Brandy.

If preferred use Pineapple Syrup in place of Maraschino.

GIN DAISY

3 parts GIN
2 parts LEMON JUICE
¾ part GRENADINE SYRUP
Slices of FRESH FRUIT
SODA WATER
½ shakerful of broken ICE

This drink is prepared in exactly the same way as Brandy Daisy on page 128, except that the Lime Juice is omitted and that the Gin is used in place of Brandy.

A very refreshing and cooling drink.

GIN HIGHBALL

6 parts DRY GIN
6 parts SODA WATER
1 slice of LEMON
1 lump of ICE

Put the lump of Ice in a tumbler and add the Dry Gin. Then fill up with Soda Water. Serve with a slice of Lemon.

This recipe can be varied by using Brandy, French Vermouth, Italian Vermouth, Port, Rum, Sherry or Whisky in place of Gin.

GINGER ALE CUP

1.1 litres (2 pints) GINGER ALE
1 tablespoon powdered SUGAR
3 parts BRANDY
1 ½ parts MARASCHINO
2 or 3 dashes of BENEDICTINE
1 ½ parts LIME JUICE
3 slices of LEMON
3 slices of ORANGE
2 sprigs of MINT
1 big lump of ICE

Put the lump of Ice into a large bowl and add the Ginger Ale. Then put in the Sugar, Brandy, Maraschino, Bénédictine and Lime Juice. Stir well and strain the mixture. Serve in a large tumbler with slices of Lemon, slices of Orange and sprigs of Mint on top.

HOCK CUP

1 large bottle of HOCK
1 ½ parts KUMMEL
3 parts BRANDY
2 parts YELLOW CHARTREUSE
1 ½ parts MARASCHINO
600ml (1 pint) SODA WATER
3 slices of LEMON
3 slices of ORANGE
Slices of FRESH FRUIT
1 big lump of ICE

Put the lump of Ice in a large bowl and add the Hock. Then add the Kummel, Brandy, Yellow Chartreuse, Maraschino and Soda Water. Stir well and strain the mixture. Serve in a large tumbler with the slices of Lemon, Orange and Fresh Fruit on top.

Some people like to add, to the above, two dashes of Bénédictine.

MINT COOLER

2 or 3 sprigs of MINT
1 dash of CREME DE MENTHE
300ml (½ pint) GINGER ALE
1 lump of ICE

Put the sprigs of Mint in a tall glass and squash with a spoon. Then add the lump of Ice, Crème de Menthe and Ginger Ale. Stir well and serve with a sprig of Mint.

A very refreshing drink.

MORNING EGG NOGG

4 parts BRANDY
1 part YELLOW CHARTREUSE
1 teaspoon SUGAR
1 EGG
1 dash of grated NUTMEG
4 parts MILK
½ shakerful of broken ICE

This is prepared in exactly the same way as Egg Nogg on page 138, except that Yellow Chartreuse is used in place of Rum.

MOSELLE COBBLER

6 parts MOSELLE
1 or 2 dashes of LEMON JUICE
3 or 4 dashes of PLAIN SYRUP
2 dashes of OLD BRANDY
1 dash of LEMON PEEL JUICE
2 slices of LEMON
½ bar-glassful of broken ICE
½ tumblerful of broken ICE

Half fill the bar-glass with broken Ice and add the Moselle. Then add the Lemon Juice, Plain Syrup and Old Brandy. Stir up and pass through a strainer into a tumbler half full of broken Ice. Serve with a dash of Lemon Peel Juice, 2 slices of Lemon and straws.

This is a long drink and is very refreshing.

MOSELLE CUP

1 large bottle of MOSELLE
1 ½ parts KUMMEL
3 parts BRANDY
2 parts YELLOW CHARTREUSE
1 ½ parts MARASCHINO
3 slices of LEMON
3 slices of ORANGE
Slices of FRESH FRUIT
2 or 3 sprigs of MINT
600ml (1 pint) SODA WATER
1 big lump of ICE

Prepare in exactly the same way as Hock Cup on page 142, but use Moselle in place of Hock.

If desired, add a dash or two of Bénédictine and serve with two or three sprigs of Mint.

NEW YORK COOLER

3 parts CANADIAN CLUB WHISKY
1 ½ parts LEMON SQUASH
3 dashes of GRENADINE SYRUP
SODA WATER
1 dash of LEMON PEEL JUICE
1 slice of LEMON
1 lump of ICE

Put the lump of Ice in a tall glass and add the Canadian Club Whisky. Then add the Lemon Squash and Grenadine Syrup. Fill up with Soda Water and stir well. Serve with a dash of Lemon Peel Juice and a slice of Lemon.

If this is sweeter than required, reduce the quantity of Grenadine Syrup.

PORT COBBLER

4 ½ parts PORT
1 or 2 dashes of BRANDY
5 dashes of PLAIN SYRUP
1 dash of LEMON PEEL JUICE
Slices of FRESH FRUIT
½ tumblerful of broken ICE
½ shakerful of broken ICE

This drink is prepared in the shaker; otherwise it is made up in the same way as the Moselle Cobbler on page 144. Leave out the Lemon Juice and use Port in place of Moselle.

A delicious and cooling drink.

PORT EGG NOGG

1 teaspoon SUGAR
4 ½ parts PORT
1 ½ parts RUM
1 ½ parts BRANDY
1 EGG
1 dash of grated NUTMEG
2 parts MILK
½ shakerful of broken ICE

This drink is prepared in much the same way as Egg Nogg on page 138, except that Port is added and the Brandy and Rum are used in different quantities.

A delicious drink.

RASPBERRY

1 ½ parts DRY GIN
¾ part LIME JUICE
1 ½ parts RASPBERRY SYRUP
2 dashes of GRENADINE SYRUP
200ml (7 fl oz) GINGER ALE
1 dash of MARASCHINO
1 lump of ICE

Put the lump of Ice in a tall glass and add the Dry Gin. Then add the Lime Juice, Raspberry Syrup, Grenadine Syrup and Ginger Ale. Stir well and serve with a dash of Maraschino.

If this is sweeter than desired, leave out the Grenadine Syrup and reduce the quantity of Raspberry Syrup.

RUM COBBLER

6 parts RUM
3 or 4 dashes of BROWN CURACAO
3 or 4 dashes of PLAIN SYRUP
1 dash of LEMON PEEL JUICE
Slices of FRESH FRUIT
½ shakerful of broken ICE
½ tumblerful of broken ICE

Prepare in exactly the same way as for Sherry Cobbler on page 154, but use Rum in place of Sherry.

This drink is very refreshing in hot weather.

RUM DAISY

3 parts RUM
3 parts LEMON JUICE
¾ part GRENADINE SYRUP
2 dashes of BROWN CURACAO
Slices of FRESH FRUIT
SODA WATER
½ shakerful of broken ICE

This drink is prepared in exactly the same way as Brandy Daisy on page 128, except that the Lime Juice is left out, Brown Curaçao is added and Rum is used in place of Brandy.

A delightful drink.

RUM EGG NOGG

4 parts RUM
1 teaspoon SUGAR
1 EGG
1 dash of grated NUTMEG
4 ½ parts MILK
½ shakerful of broken ICE

This drink is prepared in exactly the same was as Egg Nogg on page 138, except that Rum is used in place of Brandy.

This is a very popular drink.

RYE FIZZ

4 ½ parts LEMON JUICE
¾ part GRENADINE SYRUP
The white of an EGG
3 parts CANADIAN CLUB WHISKY
1 teaspoon BROWN CURACAO
SODA WATER
½ shakerful of broken ICE

Half fill the shaker with broken Ice and add the Lemon Juice. Then add the Grenadine Syrup, white of an Egg, Canadian Club Whisky and Brown Curaçao. Shake well and pass through a strainer into a tumbler. To serve, fill up the tumbler with Soda Water.

A very pleasing drink of medium strength.

SAUTERNE CUP

1 bottle of SAUTERNE
3 parts LEMON JUICE
¾ part GRENADINE SYRUP
1 ½ parts BROWN CURACAO
3 parts MARASCHINO
2 parts YELLOW CHARTREUSE
1 ½ parts BENEDICTINE
3 parts BRANDY
600ml (1 pint) SODA WATER
4 slices of LEMON
1 slice of CUCUMBER
Slices of FRESH FRUIT
1 big lump of ICE

Put the lump of Ice into a large bowl and add the Sauterne. Then put in the Lemon Juice, Grenadine Syrup, Brown Curaçao, Maraschino, Yellow Chartreuse, Bénédictine, Brandy and Soda Water. Stir well and strain the mixture. Serve with the slices of Lemon, Cucumber and Fresh Fruit on top.

If desired, you can omit the Yellow Chartreuse and the Bénédictine.

SHERRY COBBLER

4 ½ parts SHERRY
3 or 4 dashes of BROWN CURACAO
3 or 4 dashes of PLAIN SYRUP
1 dash of LEMON PEEL JUICE
Slices of FRESH FRUIT
½ shakerful of broken ICE
½ tumblerful of broken ICE

Half fill the shaker with broken Ice. Then add the Sherry; Brown Curaçao and Plain Syrup. Shake well and pass through a strainer into a tumbler half full of broken Ice. Serve with a dash of Lemon Peel Juice, slices of Fresh Fruit on top, a spoon and a straw.

A very refreshing drink in hot weather.

VERMOUTH APERITIF

¾ part BROWN CURACAO
2 parts FRENCH VERMOUTH
2 parts SODA WATER
1 small piece of ICE

*Take a wine glass and put in it the Brown Curaçao.
Then add the French Vermouth and Soda Water.
Serve with a small lump of Ice.*

> *This drink is very popular in France and is
an excellent aperitif.*

WHISKY COBBLER

6 parts WHISKY
1 ½ parts BROWN CURACAO
1 dash of LEMON PEEL JUICE
Slices of Fresh Fruit (including LEMON)
½ tumblerful of broken ICE
½ shakerful of broken ICE

Half fill the shaker with broken Ice and add the Whisky. Then add the Brown Curaçao. Shake well and pass through a strainer into a tumbler half full of broken Ice. Serve with a dash of Lemon Peel Juice, slices of Fresh Fruit on top, a spoon and a straw.

A very pleasant and refreshing drink.

WHISKY COOLER

2 dashes of ORANGE BITTERS
3 parts WHISKY
300ml (½ pint) SODA WATER
1 slice of ORANGE
1 lump of ICE

Put the lump of Ice in a tall glass and add the Orange Bitters. Then add the Whisky and Soda Water. Stir well and serve with a slice of Orange.
A very refreshing and pleasing drink.

WHISKY CRUSTA

2 parts SCOTCH WHISKY
1 part LEMON JUICE
1 teaspoon PLAIN SYRUP
1 teaspoon MARASCHINO
1 dash of ORANGE BITTERS
1 dash of ANGOSTURA BITTERS
The peel of a LEMON cut in a spiral
Slices of FRESH FRUIT
½ teaspoon powdered SUGAR
½ shakerful of broken ICE

Prepare in exactly the same way as for Brandy Crusta on page 127, but use Scotch Whisky in place of the Brandy.

Some people prefer to use Irish Whiskey in place of Scotch.

WHISKY DAISY

3 parts WHISKY
3 parts LIME JUICE
1 ½ parts ORANGE JUICE
3 parts LEMON JUICE
1 part GRENADINE SYRUP
Slices of FRESH FRUIT
SODA WATER
½ shakerful of broken ICE

Prepare in exactly the same way as Brandy Daisy on page 128, but use Whisky in place of Brandy and add Orange Juice.

If desired, add two dashes of Brown Curaçao. This improves the flavour.

WHIZBANG COOLER

3 parts DRY GIN
300ml (½ pint) GINGER ALE
1 dash of PEPPERMINT
1 or 2 sprigs of MINT
1 lump of ICE

Put the lump of Ice in a tall glass. Then add the Dry Gin and Ginger Ale. Stir well and serve with a dash of Peppermint and the sprigs of Mint on top.
This drink is very delicious and refreshing.